Joe's Be

Written by Ian MacDonald

Illustrated by Pauline Reeves

RISING ★ STARS

Joe lived on a barge. Joe's dad was a chef.
His mum was a mechanic. She was good at
fixing broken machines.

Today, Joe was helping his mum check that the lock was working. Joe loved helping to open the gates and seeing the canal boats glide through.

"Look at this cog," said Mum. "I hope I don't have to use chemicals to clean it." There was a thick layer of brown sludge on the cog.

It'll be chaos if the gates get stuck!

"It won't budge," Mum frowned. "Hand me another spanner please, Joe." Joe's mother pushed hard and, at last, the cog turned.

Well done, Mum!

That week, at school, Mrs Hedges was telling the children about how transport had changed over time. She showed them a book called *The Golden Age of Machines*.

"Before we had motorways, barges would be pulled along canals by horses. They took goods from factories to towns and villages," she said. "Imagine how slow that would be!" said Paige.

Some people live on barges.

The children looked at one another.
Joe kept quiet. He had never told his friends
he lived on a barge. They might think it
was strange.

Then, Mrs Hedges took down the old
school clock.
"This clock is the same age as some of the things
in that book," she explained.

It's not ticking!

"Sadly, it stopped ages ago," said Mrs Hedges.
Inside the clock were little cogs that had
stopped turning.
They look like the cogs at the lock, thought Joe.

"Could it be repaired?" asked Paige.

"Well, it's a bit technical," replied Mrs Hedges.

"My mum is good with technical stuff," said Joe.

"She could take a look."

Thanks, Joe!

That weekend, Joe waited by the riverbank for Mrs Hedges. He had a dull ache in his tummy.

"Oh, Joe! You live on a barge!" beamed Mrs Hedges. "How wonderful!"

Mrs Hedges stepped through the doorway with its bright badges.

Mind your head!

Thanks! I just dodged that low beam!

Mrs Hedges looked around the cabin.
Dad was in the galley, cooking on the range.

Hello, Mrs Hedges. It's nice to see you.

That's Fudge!

Joe's hamster rummaged about in his cage.

"It's just like the barge in the book," said Mrs Hedges. "Could I bring Badger Class to see it?" Before Joe could say no, his mother appeared with her tools.

That night, Joe lay awake. His tummy ache was back.

His friends all lived in homes made of bricks. What would they think about the barge?

Soon, the day of the barge outing came.
Badger Class crowded on to the arched bridge
beside the lock.
"Those are the lock gates," explained
Mrs Hedges.

"Hooray, there's Joe's barge!" chorused the children.
Slowly, the barge chug-chugged over the still water.
The class all waved, and Joe's mum and dad waved back.

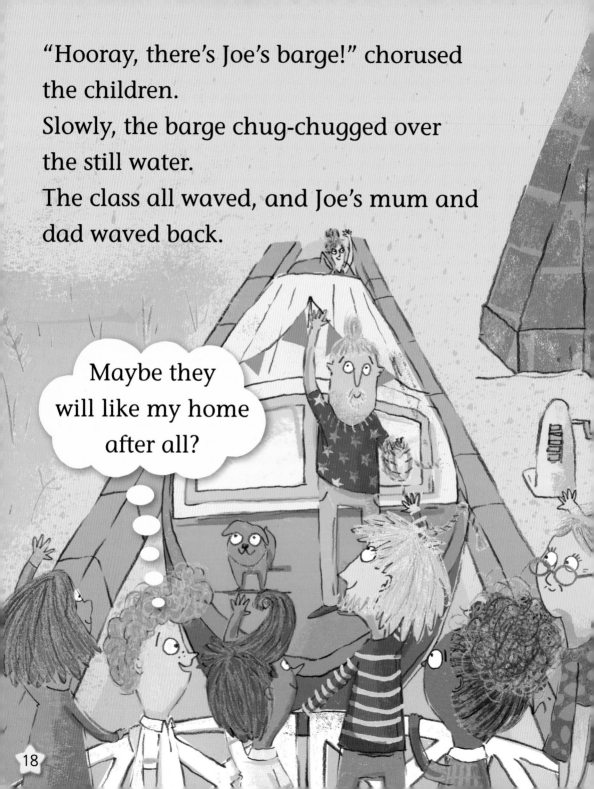

Maybe they will like my home after all?

The barge nudged its way through the lock gates. Joe's dad hopped on to the ledge and Joe helped him tie the rope to a large metal ring.

One by one, the children stepped on to the barge.

Joe's mum showed his friends around. They thought the barge was amazing.

Even Fudge enjoyed meeting everyone!
"Can I come for a sleepover?" whispered Ranjit.

After the visit, Mrs Hedges and the children said thank you. Joe's mum held up the school clock.

Joe grinned. His mum *and* his barge were brilliant.

Phonics Practice

Say the sound and read the words.

/k/	ch

school   anchor   orchestra   chemist

/sh/	ch

chef   machine   chiffon   brochure

/j/	-ge

page   age   stage   village   barge

/j/	-dge

bridge   fridge   hedge   nudge   badger

Can you say your own sentences using some of the words on these pages?

What other words do you know that are spelled in these ways?

/uh/	o

brother　mother　son　other　another

Common exception words

where　many　again　thought　through

We may say some words differently because of our accent.

Talk about the story

Answer the questions:

1 What jobs did Joe's mum and dad do?

2 What was the name of the book that Mrs Hedges showed the children?

3 Why did Joe think his mum might be able to fix the school clock?

4 How could you tell that Joe's friends liked his home?

5 Have you ever repaired something? What was it?

6 Would you like to live on a barge? Why, or why not?

Can you retell the story in your own words?